GW00675932

STATIONS
of the CROSS
OLDER for ADULTS

John van Bemmel

XXIII

TWENTY-THIRD PUBLICATIONS

Mystic, Connecticut

For age is opportunity no less
Than youth itself, though in another dress,
And as the evening twilight fades away
The sky is filled with stars, invisible by day.

Henry Wadsworth Longfellow

Twenty-Third Publications
185 Willow Street
P.O. Box 180
Mystic, CT 06355
(203) 536-2611

ISBN 0-89622-420-1

Photos: The Stations of the Cross (in St. Matthew Cathedral,
Washington, D.C.) were photographed by Louis Niznik.

Opening Prayer

God, your son never grew old. He can't teach us about getting old, can he? What can Jesus' saving death—as premature as it was—teach us about advancing years, about loneliness, about arthritis and failing eyesight, about rising costs and fixed income, about the tide of uncertainties that seems to swell over us with each year?

Even though Jesus and I do not share the experience of growing old, I know, God, that there are tender and poignant lessons for me in his last hours. His passion and death, which I celebrate in these stations of the cross, reveal above all that fullness of life is attained not by length of life so much, as by its intensity and faithfulness.

I pray these stations now, God, because I believe that Jesus will illuminate what it means to age with faith and patience, with spiritual vigor and true wisdom, with cheerfulness and generosity, with optimism and abiding hope. As Abraham and Sarah, Zechariah and Elizabeth learned, old age is a time of fulfillment and challenge, even if a time of diminishment, too. From Jesus' passion and death, I will take comfort in this all the days of my life. Amen.

Jesus Is Condemned to Death

The finality of Pilate's words seared Jesus' soul: sentenced to die by crucifixion, a criminal's death. Only hours earlier, in the stark loneliness of Gethsemane, Jesus accepted without reservation all that his Father would ask of him, "Not my will, but yours be done." Fear-filled but composed, Jesus embraced the sentence and so fulfilled his years in the loving surrender of his life.

Many people look upon old age as a fate they are sentenced to, preferring it, at least, to the alternative. They know deep down, as the saying has it, that aging is not for sissies. But to them, aging is not the common-sense course of nature but a final condemnation to eventual uselessness and absurdity. Don't they know that all creatures—stars, swans, and snakes—are born, grow old, and die? They do not value old age as an opportunity for continuing growth, but only as the fate of humans that they tolerate.

Prayer

God, by your grace, open my eyes to the true meaning of aging. Let me embrace it joyously, as my true birthright, as a challenge to develop in wisdom and grace, not as a sentence imposed on me because of my sins. Amen.

Jesus Accepts the Cross

Gethsemane fear becomes cold reality as Jesus feels the heavy beam of the cross on his beaten shoulders. What was only fear now begins to be actual pain. This burden also leaves no doubt that crucifixion is unavoidable. Whatever anticipation there may have been about his fate will now, over the next few hours, dissolve into naked reality. Jesus will accept each phase of his execution as it comes. His heart, strained with love and pain, is open to all that will follow on this path to Calvary.

Unlike Jesus, we do not enter "old age" at a set point in life. The signs of slowing down, the stronger eyeglasses, the increase of aches and pains, the loss of friends and independence—these occur gradually, at different ages, with lighter or heavier burdens for different people. But as our older years approach, and then slide by, how important it is that our minds and hearts be open to what the coming years will bring: the satisfaction and joys as well as the heartaches and pains. With the wisdom of our years, we move from fear to reality with an upbeat frame of mind.

Prayer

In Jesus' name, God, grace me to be realistic about my age. Help me to grip the reality of these years, to face my circumstances as they are, and to make the most of them. They are, Compassionate Parent, the path you have given me to come to you. Amen.

THE THIRD STATION

Jesus Falls the First Time

As often as we contemplate the weakened, weary Jesus falling to the dust, we focus on the pain of collapsing under the heavy wood and suffering still more bruises. What was most difficult and painful, in fact, was getting up. Although he was cajoled and even whipped into rising to reassume his cross and continue toward Calvary, Jesus had to rely on inner strength, on his character and motivation, to go on.

Not many people are inclined to view advancing years as a time of renewal and positive accomplishments. They see this phase of life only as going downhill both physically and psychologically. The fact is that even though the elderly may "fall" in this sense, there are many occasions when they "get up again" and go on productively with life. They can never settle for the widespread idea that old age is a time when nothing significant happens any more. There is more to each day than getting through the day. It is still a time for new insights, for personal relationships, for creative activities, for deeper wisdom and richer spirituality.

Prayer

God, by your grace, may I rise from the discouragement I sometimes feel. May I go on through these later years with a profound sense of renewal and grateful anticipation for each new day you give me to love, to create, to ponder, to converse, to learn, and to speak with you. Amen.

Jesus Meets His Mother

The sensitive, wrenching moment when Jesus' eyes met his mother's was part of his bereavement, not hers. She would soon grieve over the loss of her son, but now, the grief was his. One of Jesus' followers betrayed him; another denied he knew him; and the rest abandoned Jesus when his need was the greatest. Except for Mary and John, Jesus was alone.

It is obvious that one of the deepest sorrows of old age is increasing bereavement and the resulting sense of aloneness. Our parents die, our spouse, brothers and sisters, and even our children—perhaps the severest loss because so unexpected and "unnatural"—then our friends and others we know. Memories become more important and take up more of our day as we cling, in the only way now available, to those we knew and loved. At times, only our faith in God's presence comforts us, and the anticipation of that time when, in Thomas More's words to his daughter, "We shall meet merrily in heaven."

Prayer

God, I believe that you are with me when I feel alone, just as you were with Jesus in his lonely passion. Comfort me with the awareness that you are faithful and that your presence is forever. Amen.

Simon Helps Jesus Carry the Cross

"Why me?" Jesus heard the angry protest over the noise of the crowd. In his pain he didn't pay attention to it until a soldier brought Simon over to him. Then he understood. As Simon walked along the narrow street, he was pressed to the side to make way for the faltering Jesus and the soldiers. Just then, one of the soldiers insisted that Simon help the condemned man. "Why should I be chosen for this indignity? Why not somebody else? It's not fair!" Simon objected. Jesus understood how he felt, as Simon, for a time, took the weight of the crossbeam on his own shoulders.

The tendency to resent our misfortunes does not fade away with our advancing years. Even with the benefit of our experience and wisdom we still want to ask with indignation, "Why me?" when we break a hip or develop glaucoma. Poor Simon had more of a right to complain; he was picked at random out of a crowd. So many of our misfortunes are a natural result of getting old. Even when they seem to be "pure chance" and we want to scream, "Why me?" we have to meet the challenge and bear the unbearable if we must. Jesus understands the feelings that make us want to protest, "It's not fair!"

Prayer

Comfort me, I pray you, God. Console me when I am grieved or disappointed, especially when the hurt seems so unfair and I am singled out with no apparent reason. I honestly don't know what you can do to help me, except to fill me with a sense of your reassuring presence. Amen.

Veronica Wipes the Face of Jesus

Not many of Jesus' friends were around since his arrest the night before. Where were those who cheered him and laid palms in his path only days earlier? When it was more fashionable—and safer—not to recognize Jesus or show concern for him, Veronica steps out of the crowd to wipe his face. Did it feel cool and refresh Jesus, or did it sting his bloodied face? Either way, Jesus saw the compassionate heart that prompted her act and was grateful for it.

As people get older, their dependence on others tends to increase. More and more, people offer to help the elderly in many ways: drive them to the doctor, stop in for a chat or to see if anything is needed, or drop off some reading material. Their children, or relatives or neighbors, increasingly become caregivers. In some cases children parent their parents in costly, stressful ways. Not all offers to help are welcome, and not all "help" is really helpful, but how loving it can be to accept an offer to help or to decline an offer graciously, to speak openly and gently about what is really helpful. Like Jesus, we should look to the heart of the one who steps forward to help.

Prayer

God, I have spent a lifetime learning to be a giver, not a taker. In my later years the lesson may be to learn to be a gracious receiver. Open my heart not only to your gifts, but to the gifts—and good intentions—of those who care for me. Amen.

THE SEVENTH STATION

Jesus Falls the Second Time

Wouldn't it be understandable for Jesus to become immersed in his own suffering and fear as he falls again amid the street throng? "Who cares about these people, about Simon and Veronica who helped me, even about my mother? All I can think about is the pain I feel and the sharp sense of being so alone." With each step and each fall, Jesus is tempted to think of himself as the only one with real pain and real problems, as the only one who matters.

How easy it is—and how human—to think only of ourselves when our problems and physical ailments burn their way into our consciousness. We become absorbed with a painful hip and a lonely week and we miss the opportunity to console the recently widowed man. We forget the date we made to go shopping with a neighbor because we were pouting over a grandchild's fresh remark. The fact is, we need reminding that our usual concern for the sorrow and pain of others may help to take us out of the narrow world of our own suffering. We lighten the burden of our years when we take on the burdens of others. Was there more on Jesus' mind than his own suffering?

Prayer

God, may I never, by your grace, become so taken up with my own problems that I become blind and insensitive to the needs of others. Help me in my trials to be compassionate to those who need me, even as Jesus was, especially in his passion. Amen.

The Women Console Jesus

The small group of women approached Jesus as he struggled in the procession moving slowly toward Calvary. It was their custom as "professional mourners" to try to console the condemned man and even, we are told, offer a narcotic drink to dull the pain of crucifixion. Jesus accepts their words of comfort but, we may assume, not the drug. How well that cup must have expressed the rock-bottom reality Jesus was heading for. It symbolized more clearly than the crossbeam on his back that crucifixion was indeed just ahead. That destination, that ordeal, was inevitable.

Are we not inclined to make believe that some un-welcomed events are not really going to happen? Or to think of them as so far in the future as to be unreal? Youth, after all, thinks itself immortal, exempt from aging...until, many years later, something happens—a small event, perhaps—that brings home the cold realization that aging and death is for everyone. No exceptions. A chance comment about more gray hair, the awareness that police officers look like teenagers, the increased difficulty doing what used to be done effortlessly. Something happens, and what was vaguely true becomes here-and-now true: we're getting old. At this point in life, we have to face up to this and, like Jesus, move on in our procession toward our destination.

Prayer

God, through your grace, may I embrace with enthusiasm the realization that I am growing old. May the awareness of your presence be my "drug" to spend this stage of my life in a loving, patient, and productive way. Amen.

THE NINTH STATION

Jesus Falls Again

Perhaps at the place of execution, Jesus falls yet again, exhausted physically and emotionally. Lying on the ground, Jesus finds a moment's rest before he will have to get up to face the hammer and nails. In this moment, does he recall other times he had to get up after failure and disappointment, times when he was tempted not to pursue his mission? Does he think of missed opportunities? Are there regrets about words unspoken that might have been? People who ignored his words of life? No matter now about the past. Jesus gets up again to face the present.

An elderly person has known a lifetime of falls. Not just in the sense of "sins," but those regrets one amasses over the years: the career not chosen, the sweetheart not married, the impetuous business decision, the broken-off relationship, the hurtful words, the things that might have been. But what of those decades of wrongs and blunders now as we look back? What benefit is there in mulling over them now, engaging in self-accusation and head-shaking? "If only...." Self-forgiveness is the order of the day—every day of our later years. We have to pick ourselves up from our past and move boldly into the present. We can acknowledge the "might have beens," but we can't let them consume us.

Prayer

God, I know you have forgiven my sins. By your grace, help me to forgive myself and to put behind me for good all those regrets I have carried with me all these years. May I rise from my past and, like Jesus, be busy with what remains to be done: doing your will all the days of my life. Amen.

THE TENTH STATION

Jesus Is Stripped

Jesus is now stripped of his last possession. On a small hill just outside the city gates, Jesus stands naked to the world as the soldiers remove his clothes to prepare him for crucifixion. He has lost his strength, his freedom, his disciples, and now even his clothes. What more can he lose? But without owning so much as a garment to cover himself, he has not lost his self-possession and his dignity. Amid the degradation and torment he suffers, we see so clearly that his fundamental value and dignity come from who he is, not from what he possesses.

At a time in our older years when incomes may be fixed—even though rent, food, travel, and medical expenses are not, but rise ever higher—we may experience a wrenching worry about money and find ourselves re-evaluating what money really means to us. We need enough for decent housing and food, for recreation and medical care, and for "rainy days," but how important it is to realize, as we contemplate Jesus without a thing to call his own, that our true worth does not depend on what we own but on who we are. As we learn to do with less, we may also appreciate why the Romans said "impedimenta" when referring to their baggage. What we own has to help us to do what we should do, and not hinder us from doing it.

Prayer

By your grace, God, I want to use what I own to bring me closer to you and not to let it stand between us as so much "impedimenta." Like Jesus, I stand naked before you, and you see the core of my being, no matter how much or how little I possess. Amen.

Jesus Is Nailed to the Cross

The grotesque act of nailing a human being to a post takes place about midday, and Jesus, one of three criminals, is raised on high. Beyond the torment, the thirst, the blood loss, and the suffocation, Jesus also hears the jeers of those who arranged his execution: "He relied on God. Now let God come to rescue him."

After a lifetime of faith in God's loving presence, we still harbor in our later years a feeling that God will rescue us from the losses and pains that old age inevitably brings. We call on God, at least implicitly, to spare us from the loss of friends, the diminishment of our health, the lack of companionship, the neglect by our family. It is just as hard now as it was years ago to understand that, yes, God will rescue us ultimately, but that God will save us not from these losses but through them. God will be with us as we grow older, not spare us from the natural effects of aging. With Jesus, we trust God to be with us as we hang on our crosses, and to embrace us afterwards.

Prayer

I trust in you, God, to be with me in these declining years as you were with Jesus on his cross. By your grace, help me to live my remaining years as if everything depends on me, but to believe and to pray as if everything depends on you. Amen.

Jesus Dies on the Cross

From multiple causes associated with the crucifixion, Jesus' life is "interrupted." What did Mary and the others think as they watched Jesus surrender to the inevitable? It was the end of a loving, faithful, composed, principled, and self-sacrificing life. What if Jesus did not die at this time, but, let us say, had taught and healed and loved for another fifteen years, and then was crucified? We think, Mary's life and their lives and ours would have been so much more enriched. What if? ...But let us be content with God's ways.

The death of those we know always affects our lives. We become a bit poorer or even greatly diminished when associates, friends, or family members die. As our years increase, we lose more and more of those who have surrounded us and filled our lives. "If only my husband (wife, partner, brother, sister, friend) had not died...." We resent their deaths and perhaps blame them for our impoverishment. Our world has grown smaller and lonelier, and we are left with the faith that accepts the crooked lines of God's writing.

Prayer

God, I thank you for those you have given me to enrich my life. Help me, by your grace, to accept their passing. Though I am poorer because of it, I rejoice that they are with you and that I can smile at my memories of them. Amen.

Jesus Is Taken From the Cross

"It is finished," Jesus had said a short time earlier on the cross. Now he lay dead in Mary's arms. This emotional tableau was the model immortalized in John's Gospel and then, in marble, by Michelangelo's Pieta. Jesus' life was over. Through three decades he was the model of God for many of his contemporaries, and then, over the centuries since then, for endless millions. "He who sees me, sees the Father," Jesus had said. As the model of a human life, Jesus would touch us all and leave his blessed influence on the world forever.

Our imbedded desire to be useful does not leave us in our older years. Indeed, as time grows rapidly shorter, we keenly want to be helpful. But in our heart of hearts we also want to assure ourselves that our lives from the beginning have been useful and worthwhile, that we have influenced others for good, that the world is a better place for the love we have left in it, that we have, to some degree at least, been a model of human living. As we age, how important it is to realize that when it is time to say, "It is finished," we can look back on life as a whole and quietly nod approval.

Prayer

God, I thank you for allowing me to be your instrument to accomplish the good I have. May I, through your grace, continue to use my mind and body, my talents, and my aspirations for your purposes. Amen.

THE FOURTEENTH STATION

Jesus Is Buried

Jesus' body was removed from the execution site and brought to a tomb cut out of rock. One of those who helped prepare the body for burial was Nicodemus, the Pharisee who had questioned Jesus secretly one night a couple of years earlier about his teaching and miracles. Jesus spoke of himself as being "lifted up." Did Nicodemus connect this with being lifted up on the cross? Gazing at the lifeless body of Jesus, did he also recall that Jesus had spoken of rising three days later? Did Nicodemus believe this would happen?

Increasingly, as our years mount, we recognize the fact of our mortality. Even if we do not dwell on our death, we quietly come to grips with it. We look at Jesus' body as Nicodemus did and we ask, Did Jesus rise to new life? With faith in his resurrection we acknowledge not only our death, but our resurrection as well. We have all been "lifted up" on the cross of daily denial, separation, and disappointment, but we believe that we will rise to new life with Jesus. This faith in our ultimate victory overshadows the other joys and sorrows of our remaining years.

Prayer

God, swell my being with faith in your desire to bring me to yourself. By your grace, help me in these diminishing years to be a person of faith: faith in your continuing presence now, and faith that your eternal presence comes from my dying and rising with your son, my Lord Jesus. Amen.

Closing Prayer

God, as I step slowly along my way of the cross through the years you give me, grace me to appreciate each day's opportunities to love and to be productive, to feel your presence when I am burdened with the sorrows that accompany aging. Grace me to open my heart to your still-strange ways, to rise above my recent and long-ago failures. Grace me with the realization that you value me for what I am, and not for what I may or may not possess. Grace me, God, with the awareness that the richness of my remaining years is measured by my faithfulness to you.

God, through Jesus' passion and death, may I come to recognize that these years of both growth and diminishment will lead finally to you. I know that my way of the cross will bring me, as Jesus' did, to resurrection and to fullness of life with you forever. Amen.